LINDEN PARK
JUNIOR PRIMARY SCHOOL

Farm Animals

Turkeys

Rachael Bell

Heinemann
LIBRARY

The author would like to thank Suzannah and Freddie Wilcox for their enthusiastic help.

First published in Great Britain by Heinemann Library
Halley Court, Jordan Hill, Oxford OX2 8EJ,
a division of Reed Educational and Professional Publishing Ltd.
Heinemann is a registered trademark of Reed Educational & Professional Publishing Limited.

OXFORD MELBOURNE AUCKLAND
JOHANNESBURG BLANTYRE GABORONE
IBADAN PORTSMOUTH NH (USA) CHICAGO

Designed by AMR
Originated by Ambassador Litho Ltd.
Printed in Hong Kong/China.

04 03 02 01 00
10 9 8 7 6 5 4 3 2 1

ISBN 0 431 10084 5

British Library Cataloguing in Publication Data
Bell, Rachael, 1972–
  Turkeys. – (Farm animals)
  1.Turkeys – Juvenile literature
  I.Title
  636.5'92

Acknowledgements
Agripicture p 19/Peter Dean; Anthony Blake Photo Library pp 13 & 25/Joy Skipper, 22 (centre photo), 25; British Turkey Information Service pp 4, 11, 14, 22 (outer photos), 23, 26; Corbis pp 17/Phil Schermeister, 28/Raymond Gehman; Holt Studios p 15/Andrew Linscott; Chris Honeywell p 24; Images of Nature/FLPA pp 9/Gerard Lacz, 18/L. Lee Rue; Robert Kauffman p 7; Rouse/Elliott Photographers pp 20, 21, 27; Lynn M. Stone pp 8, 10, 12, 16, 29; Tony Stone Images pp 5/Art Wolfe, 6/Gary Moon.

Cover photograph reproduced with permission of FLPA.

Our thanks to Tony Prior, Bowers Farm, Wantage, Oxon, for his comments in the preparation of this book.

Every effort has been made to contact copyright holders of any material reproduced in this book. Any omissions will be rectified in subsequent printings if notice is given to the Publisher.

For more information about Heinemann Library books, or to order, please phone 01865 888066, or send a fax to 01865 314091. You can visit our web site at www.heinemann.co.uk

Contents

Words written in bold **like this** are explained in the Glossary.

Turkey relatives

Turkeys are large birds that come in different colours and sizes. Most farmers keep white turkeys because they grow very quickly.

Turkeys came from the **Americas**, where they lived in woods. The first people to keep them for food were the **Mexicans**, 4000 years ago.

Welcome to the turkey farm

Farmers often **rear** more than one kind of animal. On this farm, there are turkeys and a **herd** of cows.

This farmer uses part of the land for the turkeys. The rest of the farm land is used to grow **crops** and for the cows to **graze**.

Meet the turkeys

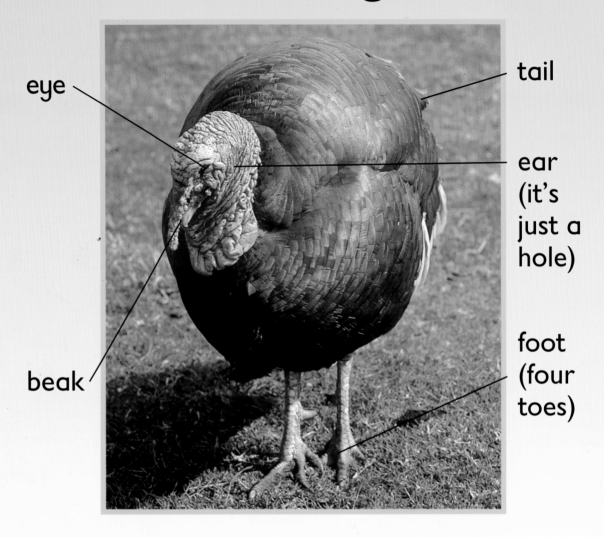

eye

tail

ear
(it's
just a
hole)

beak

foot
(four
toes)

Female turkeys are called hens.
They lay about a hundred eggs during
the spring.

snood   wattle   tail

caruncle   tassle   spur

Male turkeys are called stags. They are about twice the size of the hens. A stag can make the skin flaps on his head stretch or change colour, depending on his mood.

Meet the baby turkey

The hen sits on her eggs for four weeks. Then the **poults** peck their way out of the shell. They look bony and ugly, but soon they are round and fluffy.

This farmer buys poults from someone else. They are so small they can fit in your hand! They grow proper feathers to replace their **down** when they are 12 days old.

Where do turkeys live?

The **poults** stay under a heat lamp until they have feathers. Their box has round walls. If it was square, they would squash each other in the corners.

These turkeys live in a shed with **straw** on the floor to keep them clean and warm. A small flap leads out to the **paddock**.

What do turkeys eat?

When **poults** are inside their shell, they eat the yolk and egg white. After they **hatch**, they eat **starter crumbs** from a small **trough**.

When turkeys are outside they eat anything that is green. The farmer also feeds them special **pellets** and wheat. He gives them plenty of water to drink.

How do turkeys stay healthy?

Turkeys spend most of their time on the ground. They cannot fly properly. Running about the **paddock** gives them plenty of exercise.

Turkeys **preen** to keep themselves clean. Dust baths keep them cool and get rid of **parasites**. They flap dust over themselves, then shake it off.

How do turkeys sleep?

In the wild, turkeys **roost** in trees at night to keep safe. They grip a branch with their feet, so they don't fall off when they are asleep.

On this farm, the turkeys go inside at **dusk**. They puff out their feathers and bend their neck. They sleep like this standing on the **straw**.

Who looks after the turkeys?

The farmer and his family look after the turkeys on this farm. The children see if the turkeys need more **straw.** The farmer tops up the food and water.

The children help their father gather
up the turkeys. Turkeys keep together.
If one turkey goes inside, the others
follow.

What are turkeys kept for?

Turkeys are kept because they make good meat to eat. It is very **lean** and easy to cook. It can be used in many different dishes.

This turkey is for Christmas lunch. The turkey has been **plucked** and cooked whole in the oven. The cooked meat is then carved into slices.

Other kinds of turkey farm

Big turkey farms **rear** turkeys all the year round to send to supermarkets. The turkeys are **plucked**, then wrapped in plastic and frozen.

On large farms, the turkeys are kept in big buildings. The farmer can easily check the turkeys, and control their **temperature** and amount of food.

More turkey farms

Some turkey farms just buy turkey eggs and **hatch** them. They sell the **poults** to other farmers, who grow them to their adult size.

On these farms, machines **incubate** the eggs. That way they can hatch many hundreds of eggs. They can also check on all the poults as they hatch.

Fact file

 Poults grow very quickly. They can put on 65 grams a day – as much as they first weigh when they **hatch**!

 When a hen is sitting on her eggs, she will not leave them! The farmer has to lift her off them to feed her, and to allow the eggs to cool slightly.

 Turkeys make friendly noises to each other when they are happy. This sounds like 'gobble gobble'.

One of the heaviest turkeys on record was a Broad-breasted White that weighed 37.6 kg – about the same weight as a very heavy armchair!

 In the wild, turkeys live in separate **flocks** of stags and hens. The only time they mix is during the **mating season**. Then the stags fight each other to win the hens.

Glossary

Americas	North, South and Central America
crops	the plants the farmer grows in his fields
down	fluffy covering that newly-hatched birds have
dusk	sunset
female	the girl or mother
flock	group name of turkeys that live together
graze	nibble or eat. Cattle graze on grass.
hatch	break out of the egg shell
herd	group name for cows or bulls that live together
incubate	keep eggs warm so that they hatch
lean	very little fat in the meat
male	the boy or father
mating season	the time of year when male and female animals make babies
Mexicans	people who live in Mexico, south of North America

paddock	small field of grass which is surrounded by a strong fence
parasites	little animals that live on bigger animals and usually harm them
pellets	dry food rolled into small pieces
plucked	having the feathers pulled out
poults	very young turkeys
preening	clean feathers by gripping a feather with the beak and pulling down to the tip
rear	feed and look after young animals or children
roost	the way birds sleep
starter crumbs	food rolled into tiny pieces
straw	thick, dried stalks from crops
temperature	how hot or cold it is
trough	special food container which stops the food being spilled out or any straw or rats getting in

More books to read

Story books
I love Animals, Walker Books
Picnic Farm, Macmillan
Over in the Meadow, Walker Books

Information books
Animal Young – Birds, Heinemann Library
Images – On the Farm, Heinemann Library
The Farming Year, Autumn, Winter, Spring, Summer,
   Wayland
Mealtimes – Evening Meals Around the World, Wayland

Index